George Borrow in East Anglia

William A. Dutt

Alpha Editions

This edition published in 2021

ISBN : 9789355751911

Design and Setting By
Alpha Editions
www.alphaedis.com
Email - info@alphaedis.com

Contents

CHAPTER I
EAST ANGLIA

It is a trite saying, the truth of which is so universally admitted that it is hardly worth repeating, that a man's memory, above all things, retains most vividly recollections of the scenes amidst which he passed his early days. Amidst the loneliness of the African veldt or American prairie solitudes, the West-countryman dreams of Devon's grassy tors and honeysuckle lanes, and Cornish headlands, fretted by the foaming waves of the grey Atlantic; in teaming cities, where the pulse of life beats loud and strong, the Scotsman ever cherishes sweet, sad thoughts of the braes and burns about his Highland home; between the close-packed roofs of a London alley, the Italian immigrant sees the sunny skies and deep blue seas of his native land, the German pictures to himself the loveliness of the legend-haunted Rhineland, and the Scandinavian, closing his eyes and ears to the squalor and misery, wonders whether the sea-birds still circle above the stone-built cottage in the Nordland cleft, and cry weirdly from the darkness as they sweep landward in the night. Many a wanderer, whatever else he may let go, holds in his heart the hope that one day he may go back to the place where his boyhood's days were spent, even though it be but to dwell alone amidst the phantoms of long dead dreams and long lost loves.

East Anglia may well be compared to a sad-faced mother, who sees her children, whom she would fain keep with her, one by one go out into the wide world to seek those things that cannot be found in her humble home. For years the youths of Eastern England have had to leave the hamlet hall, the village rectory, the marshland farmstead, and the cottage home, and wander far and wide to gain their daily bread. Toil as they might, farm and field could give them little for their labour, the mother-country's breast was dry. And yet they loved her—loved her dearly. Deeply and firmly rooted in his heart is the love of the East Anglian for East Anglia. The outside world has but recently discovered the charm of the Broadland: by the dweller there it has been felt since the day when he first gazed with seeing eyes across its dreamy, silent solitudes. The secrets of the marshland wastes have been whispered in his ears by the wind in the willows, and have been sung to him by the sighing sedge. He knows the bird voices of reed rond and hover, and has read the lesson of the day's venture in the brightening sunrise and sunset glow. Amidst scenes that have little changed since the Iceni hid in the marshland-bordering woods, and crept out in their coracles on the rush-fringed meres, he is at home with Nature, and becomes her friend, her lover. She holds back no secret from him if he wills that he should learn it;

she charms him with her many moods. Her laughter is the sunlight, and ere it has died away she has hidden coyly in a veil of mist; now she is tearful with the raindrops falling on her changeful face, but the light comes back with the silvery gleaming of her winding rivers. When her lover leaves her, and wanders off to wooings far away, she reproaches him by her silence; and when he has time to think, he remembers with regret and longing the restful loveliness that was once about him like a mantle of peace.

Flowering meads, wide-reaching marshland solitudes, lonely heaths and sandhills sloping downward to the sea; wildfowl-haunted shores and flats, rivers and lagoons through which the wherries glide, the calling of the herdman and the sighing of the sea-wind through bracken, gorse, and fir ridge—these are East Anglia, and, like voices heard in childhood, they are with her children wherever they may wander, until all earthly voices are for ever lost in silence.

No one felt the charm of peaceful Eastern England more fully and deeply than did George Borrow. An East Anglian born, he was nurtured within the borders of Norfolk during many of the most impressionable years of his life, and when world-worn and weary, he sought rest from his wanderings, he came back to East Anglia to die. During his latter days, he became rather inaccessible; but an East Englishman always had a better chance of successfully approaching him than any one not so fortunate as to have been born within the compass of East Anglia. Mr. Theodore Watts discovered this when Borrow and he were the guests of Dr. Hake at Roehampton.

"When I went on to tell him," writes Mr. Watts, "that I once used to drive a genuine Shales mare, a descendant of that same famous Norfolk trotter who could trot fabulous miles an hour, to whom he, with the Norfolk farmers, raised his hat in reverence at the Norwich horse fair; and when I promised to show him a portrait of this same East Anglian mare with myself behind her in a dogcart—an East Anglian dogcart; when I praised the stinging saltness of the sea-water of Yarmouth, Lowestoft, and Cromer, the quality of which makes it the best, the most delightful of all sea-water to swim in; when I told him that the only English river in which you could see reflected the rainbow he loved was 'the glassy Ouse' of East Anglia, and the only place in England where you could see it reflected in the wet sand was the Norfolk coast; and when I told him a good many things showing that I was in very truth not only an Englishman but an East Englishman, my conquest of the 'walking lord of gipsy lore' was complete, and from that moment we became friends."

"It is on sand alone," said Borrow, "that the sea strikes its true music—Norfolk sand."

"The best of the sea's lutes," chimed in the artful Watts, "is made by the sands of Cromer."

CHAPTER II
EARLY DAYS

The eighteenth century had almost run its course when the exigencies of England's conflict with the French brought Thomas Borrow, a stalwart Cornishman, into East Anglia, on recruiting service. For several years the worthy West-countryman had served his king in the rank and file of the British army before he was appointed sergeant-major of the newly raised body of West Norfolk Militia. The headquarters of this regiment was East Dereham, a pleasant little country town situated about sixteen miles from the Norfolk capital.

Thomas Borrow came of a good Cornish family, and explanation of his having attained nothing better than non-commissioned rank is to be found in the fact that he preferred to enter the army as a private soldier—some say that he ran away from home in order to enlist. That his duties as a sergeant-major were performed in a creditable and satisfactory manner we are justified in believing, knowing that in 1798 he was raised to the position of captain and adjutant of the regiment.

While in Dereham, Sergeant-major Borrow made the acquaintance of Ann Parfrement, the daughter of a small farmer of French Huguenot extraction, living at Dumpling Green, an open neighbourhood in the outskirts of the town. This acquaintance ripened into a mutual attachment, and on Borrow receiving promotion the two were united in marriage. Two children were born to them; the younger of whom, George Henry Borrow, was born on July 5th, 1803.

The wandering instinct that George afterwards developed may well have been the natural outcome of the roving life of his early years. Before he was many months old, his parents, obedient to the dictates of military command, had moved from Dereham to Canterbury. The year 1809, however, saw them back again in the little Norfolk town with which Borrow's earliest recollections were associated.

East Dereham is a town of Anglo-Saxon foundation, and strange legends and traditions are interwoven with its history. To-day it is chiefly known for the fact that the bones of the poet Cowper rest beneath the chancel of its ancient church. To this church of St. Nicholas, George was taken by his parents every Sunday. Writing in after years, he says, "Twice every Sunday I was regularly taken to the church, where, from a corner of the large spacious pew, lined with black leather, I would fix my eyes on the dignified High-church rector, and the dignified High-church clerk, and watch the movement of their lips, from which, as they read their respective portions of the venerable

Liturgy, would roll many a portentous word descriptive of the wondrous works of the Most High."

The vicar of Dereham at this time was the Rev. Charles Hyde Wollaston. The "dignified High-church clerk" was George Philo (spelt Philoh in "Lavengro"), an old soldier, retired on a pension.

The Borrows remained in Dereham only a few months, but their stay in the place was ever after a memorable one in George's mind, for the occurrence of a great event. A young lady, a friend of the family, presented him with a copy of "Robinson Crusoe." This book first aroused in him a desire for knowledge. For hours together he sat poring over its pages, until, "under a shoulder-of-mutton sail, I found myself cantering before a steady breeze over an ocean of enchantment, so well pleased with my voyage that I cared not how long it might be ere it reached its termination."

After settling down for a time at Norman Cross in Huntingdonshire and in Edinburgh, Captain Borrow retired into private life; but not for long. Elba failed to hold the fiery Corsican, Napoleon again burst upon the battlefield of Europe, the demon of war and ravage was again abroad. Borrow's corps was levied anew, and his eldest son, John, became one of its officers. Before the regiment saw service, however, the escaped lion was again caged. But it was not disbanded, and, being in a thoroughly efficient state, was ordered to Ireland, where local trouble was feared. The autumn of 1815 saw the Borrows sail from Harwich. After a voyage of eight days, during which a terrific storm was encountered and the transports nearly foundered, the military force of eight hundred men was landed on the Irish coast. After a lengthy stay at Clonmel, where, as in Edinburgh, George was sent to school, the corps moved their quarters to Templemore.

During the following year, Captain Borrow returned to Norfolk, and settled down with his family in a small house which is still standing in Willow Lane, Norwich. George was at once entered as a pupil at King Edward's Grammar School, then conducted by Dr. Valpy, and remained a scholar there till 1818, when he attained his fifteenth year. As a schoolboy he appears to have been an apter pupil of Defoe than of the reverend headmaster of the Norwich academy. Dr. James Martineau, who was one of his schoolfellows, has related how Borrow once persuaded several of his companions to rob their father's tills, and run away to join the smugglers of the East Anglian coast. For this escapade he was awarded due punishment, which he received hoisted on the back of the future celebrated Unitarian divine. Miss Frances Cobbe, who knew both Borrow and Dr. Martineau in after years, says in her Autobiography, "The early connection between the two old men as I knew them was irresistibly comic to my mind. When I asked Mr. Borrow once to come andmeet some friends at our house, he accepted our invitation as usual, but, on finding that Dr. Martineau was to be of the party, hastily withdrew his acceptance on a transparent excuse, nor did he ever after attend our little assemblies without first ascertaining that Dr. Martineau would not be present."

On another occasion, George—probably in emulation of the East Anglian Iceni—dyed his face with walnut juice, causing Dr. Valpy to inquire whether he was "suffering from jaundice, or if it was only dirt." Dr. Jessop, who was afterwards headmaster of the school, says that there was a tradition that Borrow was indolent and even stupid. There is little doubt that he was a dreamy youth, much given to introspective thought and wild imaginings; but, in spite of these drawbacks in the dominie's eyes, he was a very human boy, fond of outdoor life and sports. Some of his pursuits, however—such as his liking for philological studies, and for the company of gipsies and horsey men generally—might well trouble his father, who was a steady-going old gentleman of strictly conventional methods and ideas. George stood in considerable awe of him, and always felt ill at ease in his presence. No doubt the old soldier frequently remonstrated with him for his indulgence in idle pleasures and lax ideas of duty. As a lad, he probably found it hard to justify himself in his father's eyes, but there is a passage in "Lavengro," written five-and-twenty years later, which clearly expresses his views:

"I have heard talk of the pleasures of idleness, yet it is my own firm belief that no one ever yet took pleasure in it. Mere idleness is the most disagreeable state of existence, and both mind and body are continually making efforts to escape from it. It has been said that idleness is the parent of mischief, which is very true; but mischief itself is merely an attempt to escape from the dreary vacuum of idleness. There are many tasks and occupations which a man is unwilling to perform, but let no one think that he is therefore in love with idleness; he turns to something which is more agreeable to his inclination, and doubtless more suited to his nature, but he is not in love with idleness. A boy may play the truant from school because he dislikes his books and study; but, depend upon it, he intends doing something the while—to go fishing, or perhaps to take a walk; and who knows but that from such excursions both his mind and body may derive more benefit than from books and school?"

Contemporary with Borrow at Norwich Grammar School were several lads whose names were afterwards written in large and shining letters on the scroll of fame. Amongst these were James Brooke, the Rajah of Sarawak, Sir Archdale Wilson, and, as has already been said, Dr. James Martineau. The old city has always borne itself with dignity during the passage of events that have gone to make up its history, as though conscious of its ability to send forth into the world sons who would do honour to her record and old foundations and traditions. From that old school they have gone out into every walk of life, carrying with them over land and sea, into court and pulpit, to bench and bar, hallowed memories of days spent within its walls. Not ten years before Borrow's name was entered on its roll, its most brilliant star had set at Trafalgar, where Nelson found amidst the hailing death that poured upon the decks of the battered *Victory* the passport to immortal fame and glory.

CHAPTER III
THE LAWYER'S CLERK

When, at the end of his fifteenth year, George Borrow completed his term of study at the Norwich Grammar School, his parents had considerable difficulty in determining upon a profession for their erratic son. In the solution of this problem he, himself, could help them but little towards a satisfactory conclusion. His strange disposition and tastes were a source of continual astonishment and mystification to the old people. What, they asked themselves, could be done with a lad whose only decided bent was in the direction of philological studies, who at an early age had attained a knowledge of Erse, and whose great pleasure it was to converse in Romany with the gipsies whom he met at the fair-ground on Norwich Castle Hill? His father was anxious that he should enter the Church; but George's unsettled disposition was an effectual bar against his taking such a step, for he would never have been able to apply himself with sufficient attention to the necessary routine course of college study.

In the midst of the warm controversy that the question excited he fell ill, and firmly believed that he was going to die. His near approach to dissolution found him quite resigned. A listless willingness to let life go, grew upon him during the dreary days of helpless inactivity. "Death," he said, "appeared to him little else than a pleasant sleep, and he wished for sleep." But a long life was before him, and, after spending weeks upon his bed, his strength came back to him, and with it the still unsolved problem of a suitable vocation. It was at last decided that he should enter upon a legal career.

There is little doubt that the legal profession was one for which Borrow was the least adapted, and of this he was well aware. When, however, in 1819, the time arrived for him to be articled to Messrs. Simpson and Rackham of Tuck's Court, St. Giles, he apparently offered no objection, and his recollections of the years when he was tied to a lawyer's desk were always pleasant to him in after-life.

But these pleasant recollections had little to do with the duties of his calling—they arose rather from the fact that his work was easy, and so intermittent as to give him ample opportunity for indulging in his day-dreams. Who can doubt the personal basis of that passage in "Lavengro" in which he says: "Yes, very pleasant times were those, when within the womb of a lofty desk, behind which I sat for some hours every day, transcribing (when I imagined eyes were upon me) documents of every description in every possible hand. Blackstone kept company with Ab Gwilym—the polished English lawyer of the last century, who wrote long and prosy chapters on the rights of things—with a certain wild Welshman, who some four hundred years before that time indited immortal cowydds or odes to the wives of Cambrian chieftains—more particularly to one Morfydd, the wife of a certain hunch-backed dignitary called by the poet facetiously Bwa Bach—generally terminating with the modest request of a little private parlance beneath the greenwood bough, with no other witness than the eos, or nightingale; a request which, if the poet may be believed, rather a doubtful point, was seldom, very seldom, denied. And by what strange chance had Gwilym and Blackstone, two personages so exceedingly different, been thus brought together? From what the reader already knows of me, he may be quite prepared to find me reading the former; but what could have induced me to take up Blackstone, or rather law?"

Yes, there was little in Borrow's nature that was in common with that of the followers of the legal profession. What food for his wild imagination could he find in the prosy records and dry-as-dust documents of a lawyer's office? They contained words that to him, as to many of his master's clients, were without meaning: his thoughts wandered beyond their mazy entanglements into a realm where the law that restrained was that of Nature alone, and whose only order was planned by the spirit that sent forth shadows and dreams. He had been too much of a rover, had seen too many strange sights in his young life, to be able to satisfy his cravings for knowledge in musty law tomes and dusty deeds. His curiosity had been aroused by many things he had seen in his early travels, he had had glimpses into so many wide fields of interest that led his mind astray. But none of these seemed to the steady-going old Militia captain to show a practical opening for his second son, whom, therefore, we find copying legal documents in a "strange old house occupying one side of a long and narrow court," instead of going a-viking with the Norseman or roving with the wild Welsh bard.

Borrow has left us a striking picture of the head of the firm of Simpson and Rackham; a picture drawn with that wealth of detail and uncompromising truthfulness which would have made the worthy gentleman tremble had he known at the time what a keen observer he was receiving beneath his roof. "A more respectable-looking individual was never seen," writes his erstwhile pupil; "he really looked what he was, a gentleman of the law—there was nothing of the pettifogger about him: somewhat under middle size, and somewhat rotund in person, he was always dressed in a full suit of black, never worn long enough to become threadbare. His face was rubicund, and not without keenness; but the most remarkable thing about him was his head, which was bald, and shone like polished ivory, nothing more white, smooth and lustrous. Some people have said that he wore false calves, probably because his black silk stockings never exhibited a wrinkle; they might as well have said that he waddled because his shoes creaked, for these last, which were always without a speck, and polished as his crown, though of a different hue, did creak, as he walked rather slowly. I cannot say that I ever saw him walk fast."

And then follows a little glimpse into the provincial life of the old Norfolk capital that shows how little change there has been in the aims and habits of a certain portion of the middle class since the first quarter of the century. "He had a handsome practice, and might have died a very rich man, much richer than he did, had he not been in the habit of giving rather expensive dinners to certain great people, who gave him nothing in return, except their company."

This worthy old gentleman must have been sorely puzzled as to what he should make of the tall, spare, serious-looking lad who was placed under his charge. He confessed to the old captain that the latter's son was "a very extraordinary youth, a most remarkable youth, indeed;" and we can well believe him. On one occasion, Borrow showed a one-eyed beggar into his master's private room, and installed him in an armchair "like a justice of the peace." At another time, when invited to Mr. Simpson's house, he electrified a learned archdeacon and the company generally by maintaining that his favourite Ab Gwilym was a better poet than Ovid, and that many of the classic writers were greatly over-valued. Borrow often distinguished himself later on by his blunt way of expressing his opinions, and the habit seems to have grown upon him early in life.

A sense of duty towards those who were responsible for his upbringing, does not seem to have been a strong point with George Borrow. He disliked the profession to which he was apprenticed, and it is evident that his mind was as absent from his duties as was his heart. He was always dreaming of sagas and sea-rovers, battles and bards. Shut up in his dull and dusty desk, he would

> "catch in sudden gleams
> The sheen of the far-surrounding seas,
> And islands that were the Hesperides
> Of all (his) boyish dreams."

No one will deny that "the thoughts of youth are long, long thoughts," for have we not all thought such thoughts, and dreamt our dreams? But they are not as a rule conducive to the attainment of a mastery of the details and subtleties of law.

One day an old countryman from the coast brought George a book of Danish ballads, left at his coast-line cottage by a crew of shipwrecked Danes. Once possessed of this work, he could not rest satisfied until he had mastered the Danish language in order that he might unearth its historical and legendary treasures. "The Danes, the Danes!" he exclaims to himself, as he holds the priceless volume in his hands. "And was I at last to become acquainted, and in so singular a manner, with the speech of a people which had, as far back as I could remember, exercised the strongest influence over my imagination. For the book was a book of ballads, about the deeds of knights and champions, and men of huge stature; ballads which from time immemorial had been sung in the North, and which some two centuries before the time of which I am speaking, had been collected by one Anders Vedel, who lived with a certain Tycho Brahe, and assisted him in making observations upon the heavenly bodies, at a place called Uranias Castle on the little island of Hveen, in the Cattegat."

No, Borrow was never meant to be a lawyer; but no calling that was possible to him could have suited him so well at the time with which we are dealing. Apparently the tasks set him were so light that he had ample opportunity for the pursuance of the philological investigations that he delighted in. His efforts in this direction attracted the attention of Dr. William Taylor, who had returned to his native city after his wanderings in France and Germany. As is well known, the accomplished scholar and translator was an intimate friend of Southey's, and it was to the poet he wrote: "A Norwich young man is construing with me Schiller's 'Wilhelm Tell,' with the view of translating it for the press. His name is George Henry Borrow, and he has learnt German with extraordinary rapidity; indeed, he has the gift of tongues, and though not yet eighteen understands twelve languages—English, Welsh, Erse, Latin, Greek, Hebrew, German, Danish, French, Italian, Spanish, and Portuguese."

Describing Taylor, when he and Lavengro are discussing together the possibility of becoming a good German scholar without being an ardent smoker, Borrow writes: "The forehead of the elder individual was high, and perhaps appeared more so than it really was, from the hair being carefully brushed back, as if for the purpose of displaying to the best advantage that part of the cranium; his eyes were large and full, and of a light brown, and might have been called heavy and dull, had they not been occasionally lighted up by a sudden gleam not so brilliant, however, as that which at every inhalation shone from the bowl of a long clay pipe which he was smoking, but which, from a certain sucking sound which about this time began to be heard from the bottom, appeared to be giving notice that it would soon require replenishment from a certain canister which, together with a lighted taper, stood upon the table beside him."

That the elderly German student and his youthful emulator were kindred spirits, there is no doubt; and Taylor seems to have instilled into Borrow's mind many of his own tastes and admirations. Amongst these was a sincere admiration for Southey, whom Borrow, with his love of superlatives, looked upon not so much as a poet as England's best prose writer, and probably the purest and most noble character to which she had ever given birth.

We have no sure knowledge of whether, while in Norwich, Borrow made the acquaintance of Old Crome. We know, however, that he was an enthusiastic admirer of the self-taught master of the Old Norwich School of artists. Still, he may never have been brought into immediate contact with him; for Crome was in his forty-sixth year when Borrow's family first appeared in Norwich, and George was then but a young lad. But before 1821, when Old Crome died, Borrow must have learnt a good deal both of the painter and his pictures, for the admiration that he afterwards expressed can hardly have been entirely the outcome of the artist's posthumous fame.

"He has painted," writes Borrow, "not pictures of the world, but English pictures, such as Gainsborough himself might have done; beautiful rural pieces, with trees that might well tempt the little birds to perch upon them; thou needest not run to Rome, brother" (this was written of the time when his brother John was leaving England to study art upon the Continent), "where lives the old Mariolater, after pictures of the world, whilst at home there are pictures of England; nor needest thou even go to London, the big city, in search of a master, for thou hast one at home in the old East Anglian town, who can instruct thee, while thou needest instruction; better stay at home, brother, at least for a season, and toil and strive 'midst groanings and despondency till thou hast attained excellence, even as he has done—the little dark man with the dark-brown coat and the top-boots, whose name will one day be considered the chief ornament of the old town, and whose works will at no distant period rank amongst the proudest pictures of England—and England against the world!—thy master, my brother, all too little considered master—Crome."

It would almost appear from the details of the dark-brown coat and top-boots that Borrow must have met Crome at some period of his Norwich life. From the foregoing eulogy, one would gather that his brother John was a pupil of the old painter. This may well have been the case, for Crome had many such pupils, amongst whom, as has lately been shown, were, in earlier years, some of the sisters Gurney of Earlham.

CHAPTER IV
DAYS IN NORWICH

The Norwich of Borrow's early years was noted for its literary and artistic associations, and the names of some of its more distinguished writers and painters were household words in the land. Harriet Martineau had "left off darning stockings to take to literature"; Dr. Taylor was opening up to English readers a new field in German writings; John Sell Cotman was making a name for himself; and Opie, who "lived to paint," was often seen at Earlham, Keswick, and in the city streets. Such names as these, and of Elizabeth Fry, Sir James Smith (who founded the Linnæan Society), and Mrs. Opie would fall upon the ear of the young lawyer's clerk whenever he mixed in polite society. The old city was then enjoying a reputation that was worthy of its best traditions; and it still prides itself on the memory of those golden days.

A bookish youth could not fail to be influenced by such associations, and it may well be that Borrow's thoughts were first drawn into a literary groove by a knowledge of what certain of these Norwich celebrities were doing. The delight he had found in the pages of his book of Danish ballads, inspired him to turn his pen from the copying of deeds to the writing of verses. His "Romantic Ballads from the Danish," printed by Simon Wilkins of Norwich, and consisting of translations from his prized volume, appeared in 1826. Dr. Jessop surmises that these translations must have brought him in a very respectable sum, but Mr. Augustus Birrell, in his own inimitable way, expresses his doubt on the point. "I hope it was so," he writes, "but, as Dr. Johnson once said about the immortality of the soul, I should like more evidence of it."

Borrow's translations and linguistic pursuits, however, were not allowed to occupy all his spare hours in those early days. Norwich and its neighbourhood had too much to show him, and to move him to reflection and enthusiasm, to allow this to be the case. By degrees, he came to love the old city, as he never got to love any other place in after-life. Writing many years later, the memories of it flooded in upon his brain until he saw its castle and cathedral, its homes and hospitality, in such a rosy light as never glowed upon the scenes through which he journeyed in after years. "Who can wonder," he asks, "that the children of that fine old city are proud of her, and offer up prayers for her prosperity? I, myself, who was not born within her walls, offer up prayers for her prosperity, that want may never visit her cottages, vice her palaces, and that the abomination of idolatry may never pollute her temples."

The grey old castle and stately cathedral were a never-failing source of interest, worship and delight to him, as they have been to many who cannot claim East Anglia for their homeland. Often he would lie upon the grass in the sunlight and watch the rooks and choughs circle about their battlements and spires. As he said, he was not formed for an indoor student, and outdoor life had ever a greater charm for him than the library or the study. Often with rod and gun (he had an old Tower musket nearly eighty years old) he would go down amongst the marshes to angle or shoot as the fancy took him and the season gave him sport. Fortunately, the old fowling-piece was sound, although condemned on account of its age, and he never came to harm by it; indeed, if we may believe him in this matter—and it is always hard to put implicit faith in a solitary sportsman or angler—he did considerable execution amongst the birds of the Broadland.

Still there were times when even the attraction of the rod and gun were not sufficient to keep him from dreaming. Then, he would throw himself down on some mossy bank and let his mind wander back into the mists and mysteries of the days of yore. There was one favourite spot of his, where, from beneath an arch, "the waters rush garrulously into a blue pool, and are there stilled for a time, for the pool is deep, and they appear to have sunk to sleep. Further on, however, you hear their voice again, where they ripple gaily over yon gravelly shallow. On the left, the hill slopes gently down to the margin of the stream. On the right is a green level, a smiling meadow; grass of the richest decks the side of the slope; mighty trees also adorn it, giant elms, the nearest of which, when the sun is nigh its meridian, fling a broad shadow on the face of the pool; through yon vista you catch a glimpse of the ancient brick of an old English hall." This old hall stood on the site of an older hearthstead called the Earl's Home, where lived some "Sigurd or Thorkild" in the days "when Thor and Freya were yet gods, and Odin was a portentous name." Earlham stands to-day as it did in Borrow's time, and, no doubt, other Norwich lads at times lie out on the hillside dreaming of the sea-rovers of Scandinavia who ravaged the hearths and homes of the marshland folk of East Anglia.

Amongst the Norwich celebrities whom Borrow met, was Joseph John Gurney of Earlham, the large-hearted Quaker brother of Elizabeth Fry. Mr. Gurney seems to have come across him one day while he was fishing, and to have remonstrated with him for taking pleasure in such "a cruel diversion." He was a tall man, "dressed in raiment of a quaint and singular fashion, but of goodly materials. He was in the pride and vigour of manhood (Joseph John Gurney was born in 1788); his features handsome and noble, but full of calmness and benevolence; at least I thought so, though they were somewhat shaded by a hat of finest beaver, with broad drooping eaves."

The worthy Quaker, whose words had the effect of lessening Borrow's inclination for angling, invited him to Earlham that he might search the library there for any such works as might please and interest him. This was an occupation so much to Borrow's taste, that we wonder he did not accept the invitation. He did not do so, however, but sought out far different companions—namely, the Romanies whom he met at Tombland Fair and on Mousehold Heath. It was many years after that he paid his first visit to Earlham. Gurney did not then remember him as the youth whom he had met by the side of the marshland stream; but he took him to the library, and showed him the books of which he had spoken many years before. One of them was the work of a moneychanger. "I am a banker myself," said Gurney, and the fact seems to have been the cause of reproachings on the part of some of the Norwich "Friends." A letter of his appears in the chronicles of "The Gurneys of Earlham," in which he writes: "I suppose my leading object in life may be said to be the bank. It sometimes startles me to find my leading object of such a nature, and now and then I doubt whether it is quite consistent with my religious pursuits and duties." Eventually he arrives at the conclusion that: "While I am a banker, the bank must be attended to. It is obviously the religious duty of a trustee to so large an amount to be diligent in watching his trust." Borrow, with whom he discussed the matter, sums up the case by exclaiming, "Would that there were many like him, amidst the money-changers of princes! The hall of many an earl lacks the bounty, the palace of many a prelate the piety and learning, which adorn the quiet Quaker's home."

It was the death of his father that brought about the first severing of Borrow's connection with Norwich. Captain Borrow, as his portrait shows and his son declares, had been a sturdy soldier, possessing great physical strength. He enjoyed several years of quiet domestic life before the end came, and lingered for some months after the fatal illness seized him. At times he would rally, so that he could walk abroad a little, or sit up in the small parlour of the house in Willow Lane, wearing an old regimental coat, and with his dog at his feet. He used to have long talks with George on such occasions, and would relate to him stories of his past life, and the distinguished people he had met. "He had frequently conversed—almost on terms of familiarity—with good old George. He had known the conqueror of Tippoo Saib: and was the friend of Townshend, who, when Wolfe fell, led the British Grenadiers against the shrinking regiments of Montcalm."

The old veteran's elder son, John, who was absent from England, hastened home just in time to receive his father's blessing. In the middle of the night, a sudden relapse brought the dying man's wife and sons to his bedside. In his last moments, his mind wandered and he spoke of "Minden, and of Meredith, the old Minden sergeant." Last of all, "he uttered another name clearly, distinctly, and it was the name of Christ." "With that name upon his lips," writes George Borrow, "the brave old soldier sank back upon my bosom, and, with his hands still clasped, yielded up his soul." His death took place on February 28, 1824, and he was buried in the churchyard of St. Giles, at Norwich.

The two brothers remained at home with their mother for some time after their father's death. John fitted up a studio in the little house in Willow Lane, and there devoted himself to his art. His work does not seem to have been very remunerative, and eventually he went abroad in connection with a mining venture, and died in Mexico in 1833. George had a great opinion of his brother's painting, and believed that if he had lived and continued to strive after excellence he would have left "some enduring monument of his powers"; but his estimate of John's endowments may have been biassed by his affection. His love for his brother was deep and abiding, and was not lessened by his father's marked preference for his elder son.

The precise date of Borrow's leaving Norwich and betaking himself to London cannot be ascertained, but it is certain that he left his brother behind him in the old home. Mr. Birrell believes it to have been not later than 1828, and says "his only introduction appears to have been one from William Taylor to Sir Richard Phillips, the publisher known to all readers of "Lavengro." Mr. George Saintsbury sums up his life in Norwich with the remark that "he occupied his time with things that obviously would not pay."

A friend of the writer, who recently examined the old house in Willow Lane, has contributed the following description of its appearance at the time of his visit:

"In a quiet, secluded court, opening from a narrow lane in the old city of Norwich, stands an unpretentious house, which at first sight presents little to attract the attention of a visitor. A closer inspection, however, discloses a marble slab affixed over the door, bearing the following inscription: 'In this house resided for some years of the earlier portion of his life, George Henry Borrow, author of "The Bible in Spain"; and other valued works. Died in 1881, aged 78 years.' The old house immediately becomes invested with great interest to one who has spent many enraptured hours over the pages of the writer whose association with Norwich has been thus commemorated by Sir Peter Eade.

"The house itself is of somewhat ancient date, and its external appearance affords little indication of its size and the comfort of its arrangement within. Its condition is practically unchanged since the time when it was inhabited by the Borrow family. The present proprietor, Mr. W. Cooper, with a commendable respect for the memory of the great author, has made but few alterations. The principal change that has been effected is in the division of the house into two separate parts. This has been easily accomplished by the simple process of blocking up a door in the hall, and forming another doorway in the front of the house. The peculiar plan of the building adapts itself to this arrangement, no other alteration being found necessary for the complete disconnection of the two parts. Of the two cottages so formed, one is at present occupied by an old couple, while the other is used as a workshop.

"On entering the front door, which has a picturesque, antique porchway, access is gained to a fairly spacious hall, paved with tiles, from which ascends the main staircase of fine old oak. The door that is now closed, opened into a commodious front room, with a large window facing the west. This contains some finely carved panelling in a good state of preservation, and was evidently the chief room of the house. From it a passage extends to the back buildings. A narrow and particularly tortuous staircase leads from the front room to the upper rooms at the back of the house, to which access cannot be gained by the main stairs. On passing through the hall, the visitor finds himself in a large kitchen, where provision is made for an exceptionally big fireplace. In common with most old houses, every inch of available space is converted into cupboards, which are to be discovered in most unexpected nooks and corners. All the rooms are panelled, but it is only the large rooms just mentioned that contain any carving.

"On the first floor, the arrangements are of a similar nature to those on the ground floor. From the landing of the main staircase open two rooms, a large one over the best room, and a smaller one above the hall. In the first-mentioned is a noticeable fireplace, which, in the place of the customary mantelpiece, has a panel-work frame, uniform with that surrounding the other rooms. The place of the centre panel was formerly occupied by a large oil painting, which remained in its position for some time after the Borrows vacated the house, and is now in the possession of Mr. Cooper. It represents 'The Judgment of Solomon,' and is supposed to be the work of John Borrow, George's artist brother. The two remaining bedrooms, which are reached by the small staircase, are of unequal size on account of a narrow passage, from which rises a short flight of stairs leading to a very irregular-shaped attic in the roof."

CHAPTER V
LIFE AT OULTON

After many painful experiences in London, whither he went in the hope of being able to gain a livelihood by devoting himself to literature, George Borrow turned his back upon the metropolis, and set out on that wild, rambling excursion narrated and enlarged upon in the pages of "Lavengro." Lapse of time has emphasised the impossibility of ascertaining how much is fact and how much fiction in the fascinating account of his wanderings. Criticism on that point is unjustifiable, for Borrow announced that the book was "a dream," and a history only up to a certain point. From what the writer has gathered, however, from those who knew Borrow intimately, he has good reason to believe that there are more facts recorded in the latter part of "Lavengro," and in "The Romany Rye," than are credited by many students of "Don Jorge's" writings.

After lengthy roamings far and wide, he returned again to Norwich, where he lived for a time a quiet life, of which he has left no record. His literary exploits had not been of such a nature as to rank his name with those of the known writers of his day; indeed, there is every reason for believing that as an author he was as little known as on the day when he abandoned the quiet little house in Willow Lane for a wider field of life. Yet, painful, and even heartbreaking, as his experiences had been, he was infinitely the gainer by the hard fate that sent him out a wanderer upon the face of the earth, and we who read his books to-day may be thankful for the tears and toilings that brought about so rich and abundant a harvest.

An introduction from Joseph John Gurney to the British and Foreign Bible Society resulted in Borrow's leaving England in 1830 for the Continent, where he went on another *wanderjahre* not unlike that he had taken in his native land.

After visiting France, Austria and Italy, we eventually find him in St. Petersburg, where he undertook the translation of the Bible into the Mandschu-Tartar language, and issued in 1835, through Schulz and Beneze, his "Targum; or Metrical Translations from Thirty Languages and Dialects." While in Russia, he made many friends amongst the nobility there, who frequently invited him to their country homes. In the same year that saw the publication of "Targum," he returned home. His stay in England, however, was a very short one. The British and Foreign Bible Society was so satisfied with his work in Russia that they pressed him to continue to serve them, and undertake a journey into Spain for the purpose of circulating the Scriptures in that country. His travels in Spain occupied over four years. While there he met Mrs. Mary Clarke, who afterwards became his wife. This lady, who was the widow of a naval officer, was connected with a Suffolk family which had been associated with the village of Oulton for several generations. Their name was Skeppar, and it was in their old Suffolk home by the side of Oulton Broad that Borrow went to live on his return to England.

Borrow, who was now in his thirty-eighth year, set to work at Oulton upon his "Bible in Spain," which was published by Mr. John Murray, three years later, in 1843. Of his method, or lack of method, in working, something may be gathered from the preface to the second edition of "The Zincali," which was written about the time of the issue of the former book. Mr. Murray had advised him to try his hand at something different from his "sorry trash" [41] about gipsies, and write a work that would really be of credit to the great firm in Albemarle Street. Borrow responded by starting on an account of his wanderings in Spain.

"At first I proceeded slowly—sickness was in the land, and the face of Nature was overcast—heavy rainclouds swam in the heavens, the blast howled amid the pines which nearly surround my lonely dwelling, and the waters of the lake, which lies before it, so quiet in general and tranquil, were fearfully agitated . . . A dreary summer and autumn passed by, and were succeeded by as gloomy a winter. I still proceeded with the Bible in Spain. The winter passed, and spring came, with cold dry winds and occasional sunshine, whereupon I arose, shouted, and mounting my horse, even Sidi Habismilk, I scoured all the surrounding district, and thought but little of the Bible in Spain. So I rode about the country, over the heaths, and through the green lanes of my native land, occasionally visiting friends at a distance, and sometimes, for variety's sake, I stayed at home and amused myself by catching huge pike, which lie perdue in certain deep ponds skirted with lofty reeds, upon my land, and to which there is a communication from the lagoon by a deep and narrow watercourse. I had almost forgotten the Bible in Spain. Then came the summer with much heat and sunshine, and then I would lie for hours in the sun and recall the sunny days I had spent in Andalusia, and my thoughts were continually reverting to Spain, and at last I remembered that the Bible in Spain was still unfinished; whereupon I arose and said: 'This loitering profiteth nothing,' and I hastened to my summer-house by the side or the lake, and there I thought and wrote, and thought and wrote, until I had finished the 'Bible in Spain.'"

Within a few weeks of the publication of the "Bible in Spain," Borrow's name was in everyone's mouth. Attempts were made to "lionise" him; but were met with his distinct disapproval, though it was always a pleasure to him to be looked upon as a celebrity. To escape from the Mrs. Leo Hunters of fashionable society, he almost immediately fled to the Continent, where he went on another pilgrimage. Having journeyed through Turkey, Albania, Hungary, and Wallachia, he again came home to Oulton, and completed "Lavengro," which had been commenced almost as soon as the manuscript of "The Bible in Spain" had left his hands. This book was finished in the summer-house of his garden by the broad where most of his future work was done, and was issued in 1851.

Defending himself against the critics who attacked him for intermingling truth and fiction in "Lavengro," he afterwards wrote: "In the preface 'Lavengro' is stated to be a dream; and the writer takes this opportunity of stating that he never said it was an autobiography; never authorised any person to say that it was one; and that he has in innumerable instances declared in public and in private, both before and after the work was published, that it was not what is generally termed an autobiography: but a set of people who pretend to write criticisms on books, hating the author for various reasons, amongst others, because, having the proper pride of a gentleman and a scholar, he did not in the year 1843, choose to permit himself to be exhibited and made a zany of in London, and especially because he will neither associate with, nor curry favour with, them who are neither gentlemen nor scholars—attack his book with abuse and calumny."

Interrogated by Mr. Theodore Watts as to the real nature of an autobiography, Borrow asked the question, "What is an autobiography? Is it a mere record of the incidents of a man's life? or is it a picture of the man himself—his character, his soul?"

This, Mr. Watts thinks, was a very suggestive query of Borrow's with regard to himself and his work. "That he sat down to write his own life in 'Lavengro' I know. He had no idea then of departing from the strict line of fact. Indeed, his letters to his friend, Mr. John Murray, would alone be sufficient to establish this in spite of his calling 'Lavengro' a dream. In the first volume he did almost confine himself to matters of fact. But as he went on he clearly found that the ordinary tapestry into which Destiny had woven the incidents of his life were not tinged with sufficient depth of colour to satisfy his sense of wonder. . . . When he wishes to dive very boldly into the 'abysmal deeps of personality,' he speaks and moves partly behind the mask of some fictitious character . . . Let it be remembered that it was this instinct of wonder, not the instinct of the mere *poseur*, that impelled him to make certain exaggerated statements about the characters themselves that are introduced into his books."

The village of Oulton lies on the border of the marshland about a mile from the most easterly point of England, and within hearing of the beating of the billows of the wild North Sea. Borrow's home, which was little more than a cottage, stood on the side of a slight rising bank overlooking Oulton Broad, and was sheltered from the winds of the sea and marshland by a belt of storm-rent pines. The house contained a sitting-room on either side of the entrance-hall, a kitchen, four bedrooms, and two attics. It was its smallness and compactness that commended it to Borrow, and it also had the extra recommendation to a man of his disposition of being quiet and secluded. Indeed, so out-of-the-way was its situation that to take a boat upon the broad was looked upon as the best and most direct means of attaining this isolated nook of the Broadland.

At the present time the broad, that stretches away from Lake Lothing to the westward of Borrow's Ham, [45] is for several months of the year picturesque with the white sails of yachts and other pleasure boats that have skimmed its placid waters since the Broadland first became a holiday resort. In the early days of Borrow's residence at Oulton, the only craft that stirred its sunlit ripples were the punts of the eel-catcher and wildfowl-seeker and the slowly gliding wherries voyaging to and from the coast and inland towns. To-day, a little colony of dwellers in red-brick villas have invaded the lonely spot where Borrow lived; but even now you have but to turn aside a few steps from the lake side to reach the edge of far-stretching marshland levels that have changed their face but little during the passage of many centuries. Farther away the marshlanders have seized upon any slight piece of rising ground to establish a firm foundation for their humble homes; here and there a grey church tower or skeleton windmill breaks the line of the level horizon. The meres and marshes have the silence of long dead years resting upon them, save where the breeze stirs the riverside reeds or a curlew cries above the ooze flats.

Queer company the "walking lord of gipsy lore" must have kept as he sat alone in that little book-lined summer-house, hearing strange voices in the sighing of the wind through the fir-trees and the distant sobbing of the sea. Out of the shadow of the past there would come to him, not only the swarthy Romanies, but Francis Ardrey, the friend of his youth; the Armenian merchant, with whom Lavengro discussed Haik; the victim of the evil chance, who talked nonsense about the *star* Jupiter and told him that "touching" story of his fight against destiny; the Rev. Mr. Platitude, who would neither admit there were any Dissenters nor permit any to exist; Peter Williams, the man who committed the unpardonable sin against the Holy Ghost, and Winifred, his patient, constant wife; the student of Chinese, who learnt the language of the land of the Celestials from the figures on the teapots; the Hungarian, who related so many legends and traditions of the Magyars; and Murtagh, with his wonderful stories of the Pope. These were the friends with whom he spent the real life of his latter days, and it is hardly surprising that under the influence of their companionship he should have become somewhat of a recluse, and lost touch with living friends and acquaintances.

Dr. Gordon Hake, whose residence at Bury St. Edmunds was contemporary with Borrow's settling down at Oulton, writes in his Memoirs: "George Borrow was one of those whose mental powers are strong, and whose bodily frame is yet stronger—a conjunction of forces often detrimental to a literary career in an age of intellectual predominance. His temper was good and bad; his pride was humility; his humility was pride; his vanity, in being negative, was of the most positive kind. He was reticent and candid, measured in speech, with an emphasis that makes trifles significant. Borrow was essentially hypochondriacal. Society he loved and hated alike; he loved it that he might be pointed out and talked of; he hated it because he was not the prince that he felt himself in its midst. His figure was tall, and his bearing noble; he had a finely moulded head and thick white hair—white from his youth; his brown eyes were soft, yet piercing; his nose somewhat of the Semitic type, which gave his face the cast of the young Memnon; his mouth had a generous curve, and his features, for beauty and true power, were such as can have no parallel in our portrait gallery, where it is to be hoped the likeness of him, in Mr. Murray's possession, may one day find a place. Borrow and his family used to stay with me at Bury; I visited him, less often, at his cottage on the lake at Oulton, a fine sheet of water that flows into the sea at Lowestoft. He was much courted there by his neighbours and by visitors to the seaside. I there met Baron Alderson and his daughters, who had ridden from Lowestoft to see him."

Borrow had many good qualities, but it must be admitted that his temper was queer and uncertain. At times he was passionate and overbearing, and he never had the necessary patience to submit to what seemed to him the inanities and boredom of admirers, hero worshippers, and others who were desirous of being brought to his notice. Mr. J. W. Donne, who occupied the position of librarian of the London Library and was afterwards reader of plays, related to Dr. Hake how on one occasion Miss Agnes Strickland urged him to introduce her to her brother author. Borrow, who was in the room at the time, offered some objection, but was at length prevailed upon to accept the introduction. Ignorant of the peculiar twists in Borrow's nature, the gifted authoress commenced the conversation by an enthusiastic eulogy of his works, and concluded by asking permission to send him a copy of her "Queens of England." "For God's sake, don't, madam," exclaimed Borrow. "I should not know what to do with them." He then got up in a rage, and, addressing Mr. Donne, said, "What a d--- fool that woman is!"

"He once," writes Dr. Hake, "went with me to a dinner at Mr. Bevan's country-house, Rougham Rookery, and placed me in an extremely awkward position. Mr. Bevan was a Suffolk banker, a partner of Mr. Oakes. He was one of the kindest and most benevolent of men. His wife was gentle, unassuming, attentive to her guests. A friend of Borrow, the heir to a very considerable estate, had run himself into difficulties and owed money, which was not forthcoming, to the Bury banking-house; and in order to secure repayment Mr. Bevan was said to have 'struck the docket.' I knew this beforehand from Borrow, who, however, accepted the invitation, and was seated at dinner at Mrs. Bevan's side. This lady, a simple, unpretending woman, desirous of pleasing him, said, 'Oh, Mr. Borrow, I have read your books with so much pleasure!' On which he exclaimed, 'Pray, what books do you mean, madam? Do you mean my account-books?' On this he fretted and fumed, rose from the table, and walked up and down amongst the servants during the whole of dinner, and afterwards wandered about the rooms and passage, till the carriage could be ordered for our return home."

On another occasion Hake and Borrow were guests together at Hardwicke House, Suffolk, a fine old Jacobean Hall, then the residence of Sir Thomas Cullum. There were also staying at the Hall at the time Lord Bristol, Sir Fitzroy Kelly, William Makepeace Thackeray, and other distinguished people. Borrow and Thackeray did not get on well together. The latter evidently felt it his duty to live up to his reputation by entertaining the company with lively sallies and witticisms. At last he approached Borrow, and inquired, "Have you read my Snob Papers in *Punch*?" "In *Punch*?" asked Borrow. "It is a periodical I never look at."

Mr. John Murray, in his "Reminiscences," has also given instances of Borrow's strange behaviour in other people's houses; but there is reason to believe that he often keenly reproached himself afterwards for giving way in public to such unseemly displays of temper and spleen. That his heart was in the right place and he was not lacking in powers of restraint, are facts fully demonstrated by the following incident. He was invited to meet Dr. Robert Latham at the house of Dr. Hake, who had many inward tremors at what might be the outcome of bringing them together. Latham was in the habit of indulging somewhat too freely at table, and under such circumstances, as might be expected, was often deficient in tact and courtesy.

"All, like most things that are planned, began well. But with Latham life was a game of show. He had to put forth all his knowledge of subjects in which he deemed Borrow was an adept. He began with horse-racing. Borrow quietly assented. He showed off all he knew of the ring. Borrow freely responded. He had to show what he knew of publishers, instancing the Longmans. Borrow said, 'I suppose you dine with your publishers sometimes?' It was Latham's opportunity; he could not resist it, and replied, 'Never; I hope I should never do anything so low. You do not dine with Mr. John Murray, I presume?' 'Indeed, I do,' said Borrow, emotionally. 'He is a most kind friend. When I have had sickness in my house he has been unfailing in his goodness towards me. There is no man I value more.' Latham's conversation was fast falling under the influence of wine; with this his better taste departed from him. 'I have heard,' he said, 'that you are a brave man over a bottle of wine. Now, how many bottles can you get through at a sitting?' Borrow saw what the other was; he was resolved not to take offence at what was only impertinent and self-asserting, so he said, 'When I was in Madrid I knew a priest who would sit down alone to his two bottles.' 'Yes,' replied Latham, with his knowing look and his head on one side like a bird, 'but what I want to know is, how many bottles you can manage at one sitting?' 'I once knew another priest,' said Borrow, 'it was at Oporto; I have seen him get through two bottles by himself.' By this time Latham was a little unsteady, he slipped from his chair as if it had been an inclined plane and lay on the carpet. He was unable to rise, but he held his head up with a cunning smile, saying, 'This must be a very disreputable house.' Borrow saw Latham after this at times on his way to me, and always stopped to say a kind word to him, seeing his forlorn condition."

Given as he was to snubbing and browbeating others, Borrow was not a man to sit silent and see another man badly treated without raising hand or voice in his defence. Proof of this is found in an instructive story related by Mr. J. Ewing Ritchie in his chatty "East Anglian Reminiscences." "One good anecdote I heard about George Borrow," writes Mr. Ritchie. "My informant was an Independent minister, at the time supplying the pulpit at Lowestoft and staying at Oulton Hall, then inhabited by a worthy dissenting tenant. One night a meeting of the Bible Society was held at Mutford Bridge, at which the party from the Hall attended, and where George Borrow was one of the speakers. After the meeting was over, all the speakers went back to supper at Oulton Hall, and my friend among them, who, in the course of the supper, found himself violently attacked by a clergyman for holding Calvinistic opinions. Naturally my friend replied that the clergyman was bound to do the same. 'How do you make that out?' 'Why, the Articles of your Church are Calvinistic, and to them you have sworn assent!' 'Oh yes, but there is a way of explaining them away!' 'How so?' said my friend. 'Oh,' replied the clergyman, 'we are not bound to take the words in their natural sense.' My friend, an honest, blunt East Anglian, intimated that he did not understand that way of evading the difficulty; but he was then a young man and did not like to continue the discussion further. However, George Borrow, who had not said a word hitherto, entered into the discussion, opening fire on the clergyman in a very unexpected manner, and giving him such a setting down as the hearers, at any rate, never forgot. All the sophistry about the non-natural meaning of terms was held up by Borrow to ridicule, and the clergyman was beaten at every point. 'Never,' says my friend, 'did I hear one man give another such a dressing as on that occasion.'"

Borrow was often asked by visitors to Oulton if it was his intention to leave behind him the necessary material for the compilation of a biography of his strange career. This, however, he could never be persuaded to do. He maintained that "Lavengro," "The Romany Rye," and "The Bible in Spain," contained all of his life that it was necessary for posterity to know. It was not the man but his works that should live, he would say, and his books contained the best part of himself. While in London, however, at the house which he took in Hereford Square, Brompton, he consented to sit for his portrait, the artist being Henry Philips. This picture afterwards passed into the possession of his step-daughter, Mrs. Henrietta MacOubrey.

Of the painting of this portrait a very good story is told. Borrow was a very bad sitter, he was ever anxious to get out into the fresh air and sunlight. Philips was greatly hindered by this restlessness, but one day he hit upon a plan which conquered the chafing child of Nature and served his own purpose admirably. He was aware of Borrow's wonderful gift of tongues and the fascination that philological studies had for him. So he remarked, "I have always heard, Mr. Borrow, that the Persian is a very fine language; is it so?" "It is, Philips; it is," replied "Lavengro." "Perhaps you will not mind reciting me something in the Persian tongue?" "Dear me, no; certainly not." And then Borrow's face lit up with the light that Philips longed for, and he commenced declaiming at the top of his voice, while the painter made the most of his opportunity. When he found his subject was lapsing into silence, and that the old feeling of weariness and boredom was again creeping upon him, he would start him off again by saying, "I have always heard that the Turkish—or the Armenian—is a very fine language," with a like result, until at length the portrait was completed.

The monotony of Borrow's life at Oulton was varied by occasional visits to London and excursions into Wales and to the Isle of Man. In his travels through Wales he was accompanied by his wife and step-daughter. How the journey was brought about he explains in the first chapter of "Wild Wales," a work which, published in 1862, was the outcome of his ramblings in the Principality. "In the summer of 1854, myself, wife and daughter, determined upon going into Wales, to pass a few months there. We are country-people of a corner of East Anglia, and, at the time of which I am speaking, had been residing so long on our own little estate that we had become tired of the objects around us, and conceived that we should be all the better for changing the scene for a short period. We were undetermined for some time with respect to where we should go. I proposed Wales from the first, but my wife and daughter, who have always had rather a hankering after what is fashionable, said they thought it would be more advisable to go to Harrogate or Leamington. On my observing that these were terrible places for expense, they replied that though the price of corn had of late been shamefully low we had a spare hundred pounds or two in our pockets and could afford to pay for a little insight into fashionable life. I told them that there was nothing I so much hated as fashionable life, but that, as I was anything but a selfish person, I would endeavour to stifle my abhorrence of it for a time and attend them either to Leamington or Harrogate. By this speech I obtained my wish, even as I knew I should, for my wife and daughter instantly observed that, after all, they thought we had better go into Wales, which, though not so fashionable as either Leamington or Harrogate, was a very picturesque country, where they had no doubt they should get on very well, more especially as I was acquainted with the Welsh language."

This is Borrow's account of how he obtained his own way; it would have been interesting had his wife and step-daughter also recorded their version of the affair.

Borrow's mother, who had given up her house in Willow Lane, died at Oulton, in 1860. The same year Borrow published a small volume, entitled "The Sleeping Bard," a translation from the Welsh of Elis Wyn. During the years 1862–3 various translations of his appeared in *Once a Week*, a magazine that then numbered amongst its contributors such writers as Harriet Martineau and S. Baring-Gould, and artists as Leech, Keene, Tenniel, Millais and Du Maurier. Amongst these translations were "The Hailstorm, or the Death of Bui," from the ancient Norse; "The Count of Vendal's Daughter," from the ancient Danish; "Harald Harfagr," from the Norse; "Emelian the Fool," and "The Story of Yashka with the Bear's Ear," from the Russian; and several ballads from the Manx. Other translations from the Danish of Oehlenschlaeger are still in the possession of Mrs. MacOubrey, and have never been printed. His last book, "The Romano Lavo-Lil," was issued in 1872.

Between 1860 and 1870, Borrow spent a good deal of his time in London, at his house in Hereford Square. This was mainly on account of the ill-health of his wife, who died there in 1869, and was buried in Brompton Cemetery. After her death, however, he returned to Oulton, telling Mr. Watts that he was going down into East Anglia to die.

From that time his life was lived more apart from the world than ever. His visitors were few; and fewer still were the visits he paid to others. During his latter years his tall, erect, somewhat mysterious figure was often seen in the early hours of summer mornings or late at night on the lonely pathways that wind in and out from the banks of Oulton Broad. He loved to be mysterious, and the village children used to hush their voices and draw aside at his approach. They looked upon him with fear and awe—for had they not seen him stop and talk with the gipsies, who ran away with little children? But in his heart, Borrow was fond of the little ones, though it amused him to watch the impression his strange personality made upon them. Older people he seldom spoke to when out on his solitary rambles; but sometimes he would flash out such a glance from beneath his broad-brimmed hat and shaggy eyebrows as would make timid country-folk hasten on their way filled with vague thoughts and fears of the evil eye. Mr. John Murray has referred to this love of mystery on the part of his father's friend, and also to his moody and variable temperament; while Mr. G. T. Bettany has related how he enjoyed creating a sensation by riding about on a fine Arab horse which he brought home with him from Turkey in 1844.

Still Borrow was not unpopular with the villagers, many of whom, long after his death, remembered little acts of kindness on his part by which they had benefited. To the sick and infirm he was always a good friend, though his almost invariable remedy for all the ills that flesh is heir to were wine and ale. He was exceedingly fond of animals, and nothing aroused his wrath more than to see them badly treated. On one occasion, while out walking not far from his home, he encountered some men who were ill-using a fallen horse. He remonstrated with them, and his words, backed by his commanding figure, prevailed upon them to desist from their cruelty. He then sent one of them for a bowl of ale. When it was brought, he knelt down on the road beside the exhausted animal, and poured it down its throat. Having afterwards assisted the men in getting the horse upon its feet, he left them, but not before he had given them a severe lecture on the treatment of dumb animals in general and fallen horses in particular.

At another time, a favourite old cat that was ill, crawled out of his house to die in the garden hedge. Borrow no sooner missed the poor creature than he went in search of it, and brought it indoors in his arms. He then laid it down in a comfortable spot, and sat and watched it till it was dead.

Owing to the somewhat eccentric manner in which he passed his latter days, there were some persons who assumed after his death that in his declining years he lacked the attention of friends, and the little comforts and considerations that are due to old age. Yet this was not so; if the world heard little of him from the time of his final retirement into rural seclusion, and lost sight of him and believed him dead, it was his own choosing that they should remain in ignorance. He had had his day, a longer and fuller one than falls to the lot of most of the sons of men, and, when the weight of years began to tell upon him, he chose to live out the little time that was left to him amidst such scenes as were in harmony with his nature. He died at Oulton on July 26, 1881, just three weeks after the completion of his seventy-eighth year. His step-daughter, Mrs. MacOubrey, the Henrietta of "Wild Wales," who had a sincere affection for him, was his constant attendant during his last illness, and was with him at the end. He was buried at Brompton

Cemetery, where his body lies beside that of his wife. Not long after his death, his Oulton home was pulled down. All that now remains to mark the spot where it once stood are the old summer-house in which he loved to linger, and the ragged fir-trees that sighed the requiem of his last hours.

CHAPTER VI
BORROW AND PUGILISM

During the first quarter of the present century pugilism was rampant in the Eastern Counties of England. A pugilistic encounter was then looked upon as an affair of national interest, and people came in their thousands from far and near to witness it. The Norwich neighbourhood was noted for its prize-fights, and Borrow had the names of all the champions at his tongue's end. Cobbett, Cribb, Belcher, Tom Spring of Bedford, Black Richmond, Irish Randall—he was acquainted with the records of them all, as well as with those of the leading fighting-men amongst the gipsies. They were to him the leaders of the old spirit of English aggressiveness, and as such he revered them. His pen was always ready to defend a straightforward bruiser, with whom, he contended, the Roman gladiator and the Spanish bull-fighter were not to be compared. He, himself, was no mean student of the art of self-defence, and there is some ground for believing that the scene between Lavengro and the Flaming Tinman, in which the burly tinker succumbs to the former's prowess after a warm encounter in the Mumpers' Dingle, is founded upon an event which occurred during Borrow's wayward progress through rural England.

On the publication of "Lavengro," Borrow's evident partiality for the pugilists of his day brought down upon him a torrent of criticism and condemnation. Who, it was asked, but a man of coarse instincts could have found pleasure in mingling with brutal fighting-men and describing their desperate exploits? The writer of a work who went out of his way to drag in such characters and scenes as these could be little better than a barbarian!

Borrow was not a man to sit down quietly under such attacks as these; he waited his opportunity, and then had his fling. At the end of "The Romany Rye," there appeared an Appendix, in which the author set himself the task of smashing his critics. This same Appendix is an amazing piece of writing; in it Borrow slashes right and left as might a gallant swordsman who found himself alone in the midst of a mob bent on his destruction. Mr. Augustine Birrell regrets that it was ever printed; but there are few who will agree with him; it contains too many good things that Borrovians would be loth to lose.

Borrow's defence is carried on in his own peculiar and inimitable style, it is an onslaught into the camp of the enemy. Speaking of the prize-fighters, whom a reviewer condemned as blackguards, he exclaims defiantly, "Can the rolls of the English aristocracy exhibit names belonging to more noble, more heroic men than those who were called respectively Pearce, Cribb, and Spring? Did ever one of the English aristocracy contract the seeds of fatal consumption by rushing up the stairs of a burning edifice, even to the topmost garret, and rescuing a woman from seemingly inevitable destruction? The writer says no. A woman was rescued from the top of a burning house; but the man who rescued her was no aristocrat; it was Pearce, not Percy, who ran up the burning stairs." And so he goes on, overwhelming his opponents with a tornado of generalities that have nothing whatever to do with prize-fighting, and yet how delightful it all is!

There were other critics—Borrow always had plenty of critics—who found it difficult to make his admiration for the prize-ring fit in with his denunciation in one passage of "those disgraceful and brutalising exhibitions called pugilistic combats." The explanation has been suggested that for once the "John Bull" Borrow, with his patriotic exaltation of all things English, gave way before the proselytising agent of the British and Foreign Bible Society. It would be hard to find a writer who does not contradict himself at times, and Borrow was so much a man of "moods" that it would be uncharitable to set him down as a hypocrite, as Caroline Fox does, because all his sayings and doings do not tally with a superhuman exactitude.

But whether it was in respect to the number of glasses of ale that he drank on his Welsh rambles—and has not "Wild Wales" been called "The Epic of Ale?"—or his associations with the great fighting-men of his day, he was never ashamed to admit his liking both for the ale and the men. "Why should I hide the truth?" he asks, when telling of his presence when a boy of fourteen at a prize-fight which took place near Norwich. Thurtell, whose boast it was that he had introduced bruising into East Anglia, had arranged the fight, which was ever after memorable to Borrow for the appearance on the scene of Gipsy Will and his celebrated gang. This well-known Romany, who was afterwards hanged outside the gaol at Bury St. Edmunds for a murder committed in his youth, was a sturdy, muscular fellow, six feet in height, who rendered himself especially noticeable by wearing a broad-brimmed, high-peaked Andalusian hat. He was anxious on this occasion to fight the best man in England for twenty pounds (not a very tempting sum in the light of our more advanced days); but no one accepted the challenge, though a young countryman was anxious to do so until assured by his friends that the notorious gipsy would certainly kill him.

Borrow has gone out of his way in "The Gipsies of Spain" to give a full description of this Gipsy Will and his notable companions. At the risk of wearying some readers who deprecate the prize-ring and its cosmopolitan environment, the writer quotes something of this description, as it appears in one of the less known of Borrow's works:

"Some time before the commencement of the combat, three men, mounted on wild-looking horses came dashing down the road in the direction of the meadow, in the midst of which they presently showed themselves, their horses clearing the deep ditches with wonderful alacrity. 'That's Gipsy Will and his gang,' lisped a Hebrew pickpocket; 'we shall have another fight.' The word gipsy was always sufficient to excite my curiosity, and I looked attentively at the new-comers.

"I have seen gipsies of various lands, Russian, Hungarian, and Turkish; and I have also seen the legitimate children of most countries of the world; but I never saw, upon the whole, three more remarkable individuals, as far as personal appearance was concerned, than the three English gipsies who now presented themselves to my eyes on that spot. Two of them had dismounted, and were holding their horses by the reins. The tallest, and, at the first glance, the most (!) interesting of the two, was almost a giant, for his height could not have been less than six feet three. It is impossible for the imagination to conceive anything more perfectly beautiful than were the features of this man, and the most skilful sculptor of Greece might have taken them as his model for a hero and a god. The forehead was exceedingly lofty, a rare thing in a gipsy; the nose less Roman than Grecian, fine, yet delicate; the eyes large, overhung with long drooping lashes, giving them almost a melancholy expression; it was only when the lashes were elevated that the gipsy glance was seen, if that can be called a glance which is a strange stare, like nothing else in the world. His complexion was a beautiful olive; and his teeth were of a brilliancy uncommon even among these people, who have all fine teeth. He was dressed in a coarse waggoner's slop, which, however, was unable to conceal altogether the proportions of his noble and Herculean figure. He might be about twenty-eight. His companion and his captain, Gipsy Will, was, I think, fifty, when he was hanged ten years subsequently. I have still present before me his bushy black hair, his black face, and his big black eyes, fixed and staring. His dress consisted of a loose blue jockey coat, jockey boots and breeches; in his hand was a huge jockey whip, and on his head (it struck me at the time for its singularity) a broad-brimmed, high-peaked, Andalusian hat, or at least one very much resembling those generally worn in that province. In stature he was shorter than his more youthful companion, yet he must have measured six feet at least, and was stronger built, if possible. What brawn! what bone! what legs! what thighs! The third gipsy, who remained on horseback, looked more like a phantom than anything human. His complexion was the colour of pale dust, and of that same colour was all that pertained to him, hat and clothes. His boots were dusty, of course, and his very horse was of a dusty dun. His features were whimsically ugly, most of his teeth were gone, and as to his age, he might be thirty or sixty. He was somewhat lame and halt; but an unequalled rider when once upon his steed, which he was naturally not very solicitous to quit. I subsequently discovered that he was considered the wizard of the gang."

Any one who is familiar with the living descendants of the Romanies of Borrow's early lifetime will know that amongst the few characteristics of their fathers that have been preserved down to the present day is that skill at boxing or fisticuffs which was an absolute necessity in a time when their hand was against every man and every man's hand against them. Nearly all the male Romanies are possessed of a lithe, sinewy, active frame, combined with a quickness of hand and eye that gives them a considerable advantage over less alert antagonists of heavier build. They are not, as a rule, in a hurry to come to blows, for they know that in the event of injury or police-court proceedings resulting from an encounter, prejudice is strongly against the gipsy. Still, the Romany blood pulses quickly, and when it flies to the swarthy cheek and sets the eyes flashing, the time has come for someone to beware. The writer has seen something of the gipsy's skill and adroitness under such conditions, and the impression made was a lasting one. He has known, too, of a small, slim-built Romany thrashing a strong, six-feet-high constable, for unwarrantable interference with the former's mother in a public bar. The Romany race is fast dying out from our midst; but it is dying what the sportsman would call "game."

Although Borrow's obvious admiration for the brawny men of the prize-ring brought him almost universal condemnation, his opinions were unchanged by his critics' wrath and denunciations. There were many points in his father's character for which he held him in esteem and affection; but he admired him most because he had once vanquished Big Ben Brain in a fight in Hyde Park.

"He was always at his best," writes Mr. Theodore Watts, "in describing a pugilistic encounter; for in the saving grace of pugilism as an English accomplishment, he believed as devoutly as he believed in East Anglia and the Bible."

CHAPTER VII
BORROW AND THE EAST ANGLIAN GIPSIES

East Anglia has for centuries been a favourite roaming ground for certain of the families of the true Romany tribe. The reason for this, assigned by the gipsies themselves, is not a flattering one to East Englanders. They will tell you, if you are in their confidence, that they come to East Anglia on account of the simplicity and gullibility of its inhabitants. Nowhere else can the swarthy *chals* find *gorgios* so ready to purchase a doctored nag, or the dark-eyed *chis* so easily cozen credulous villagers and simple servant-girls by the mysteries of *dukkeripen.* Every fair-ground and race-course is dotted with their travelling vans; the end of every harvest sees them congregate on the village greens; the "making up" of the North Sea fishing-boats attracts them to the Eastern coast.

It may well be that Borrow first made the acquaintance of the Romanies when a child at East Dereham, for there is a heath just outside the little town which has long been their central halting-place for the district. If this was the case, he has left no record of such a meeting: in all probability, had his wondering eyes rested upon their unfamiliar faces and smouldering camp-fires he would have shared the childish fears instilled by kitchen and nursery legends and have fled the scene. It was outside Norman Cross that he first came into close contact with the alien wanderers. Straying into a green lane he fell in with a low tent from which smoke was issuing, and in front of which a man was carding plaited straw, while a woman was engaged in the manufacture of spurious coin. Their queer appearance, so unlike that of any men or women he had hitherto encountered, excited his lively curiosity; but, ere he had time to examine them closely, they were down upon him with threats and curses. Violence was about to be done to him when a viper, which he had concealed in his jacket, lifted its head from his bosom, and the gipsies' wrath at being discovered changed to awe of one who fearlessly handled such a deadly creature. From that day Borrow's interest in the Romany tribe continued to widen and deepen, until, at length, when fame and fortune were his, it led him to take extended journeys into Hungary, Wallachia, and other European countries for the purpose of searching out the descendants of the original wanderers from the East and learning from them their language, customs and history.

Borrow himself says that he could remember no time when the mere mention of the name of gipsy did not awaken within him feelings hard to be described. He could not account for it, but some of the Romanies, he remarks, "to whom I have stated this circumstance have accounted for it on the supposition that the soul which at present animates my body has at some former period tenanted that of one of their people, for many among them are believers in metempsychosis and, like the followers of Bouddha, imagine that their souls by passing through an infinite number of bodies, attain at length sufficient purity to be admitted to a state of perfect rest and quietude, which is the only idea of heaven they can form."

The Norwich Castle Hill provided Borrow with many opportunities of observing the habits of the East Anglian Romanies, who, in his day, attended in considerable numbers the horse sales and fairs that were held in the old city. Thither would come the Smiths or Petulengros, Bosviles, Grays and Pinfolds; and often, when they left the Hill, he would accompany them to their camps on Mousehold Heath and to neighbouring fairs and markets. Their daring horsemanship fascinated him, while the strange tongue they employed amongst themselves when bargaining with the farmers and dealers, aroused in him a curiosity that could only be satisfied by a closer acquaintance with its form and meaning. Many of the *chals* and *chis* to be met with in "Lavengro" and "The Romany Rye" were transferred to the pages of those works from the East Anglian heaths and fairsteads. It was on a heath not far from his Suffolk home that he introduced the Jew of Fez to Jasper Petulengro in order that he might refute the theory entertained by one of his critics that the Romanies were nothing less than the descendants of the two lost tribes of Israel.

The village of Oulton, too, gave him many chances of intercourse with the gipsies. Within five minutes' walk of his home there is a spot where they frequently assembled, and where a few of them may sometimes be seen even at the present day. The writer has reason to know that the gipsies looked upon Borrow with no small amount of curiosity, for they were unaccustomed to meet with *gorgios* of his position who took so keen an interest in their sayings and doings. As a rule, they are exceedingly suspicious of the approaches of any one outside the Romany pale; and it must not be assumed that he was popular with them because he usually succeeded in extracting from them the information he required. There was something about Borrow that made it hard to evade his questioning; he had such a masterful way with him, and his keen eyes fixed upon a man as though they would pierce him through and read his most secret thoughts. He himself attributes his success with the gipsies to his knowledge of the Romany tongue and customs, while they firmly believed that he had gipsy blood in his veins. "He has known them," he says, writing of himself as the author of "The Zincali," "for upwards of twenty years in various countries, and they never injured a hair of his head or deprived him of a shred of his raiment; but he is not deceived as to the motive of their forbearance: they thought him a *Rom*, and on this supposition they hurt him not, their love of 'the blood' being their most distinguishing characteristic." This error on their part served his purpose well, as it enabled him to obtain from them a great deal of curious knowledge that would never have come into his possession had it been known he was one of the despised *gorgios*. He was known amongst them as the Romany Rye; but that is a name by which, even at the present day, they distinguished any stranger who can "rokkra Romany" to the extent of a dozen words.

Although Borrow spent so much time amongst the East Anglian gipsies, it is often difficult to ascertain the exact localities in which he met with them. He seldom condescends to give the date of any incident, and as infrequently does he choose to enlighten us as to his precise whereabouts when it occurred. Then, too, one might conclude that his investigations were almost wholly confined to two families, those of the Smiths or Petulengros, and Hernes. As Mr. Watts has aptly remarked, one would imagine from all that is said about these families in "Lavengro" and "The Romany Rye" that he knew nothing about the other Romanies of the Eastern Counties. Yet he must have been familiar also with the Bosviles, Grays, and Pinfolds, some descendants of whom still haunt the heaths and greens of Eastern England. According to Borrow, the Petulengros were continually turning up wherever he might wander. Jasper Petulengro's nature seems something akin to that of the Wandering Jew; and yet, if we may believe "Lavengro" and our own knowledge, the Smiths look upon East Anglia as their native heath. First, he appears in the green lane near Norman Cross; then at Norwich Fair and on Mousehold Heath; again at Greenwich Fair, where he tries to persuade Lavengro to take to the gipsy life; and once more in the neighbourhood of the noted dingle of the Isopel Berners episode. This, of course, is due to the exigencies of what Mr. Watts calls a "spiritual biography," and it is evident that whenever anything particularly striking pertaining to the Romanies occurs to Borrow the Romanies themselves promptly appear to illustrate it.

Yet we know that Jasper Petulengro was a genuine character, even if he comes to us under a fictitious name. He was a representative of one of the oldest of the East Anglian gipsy families, and a personal friend of Borrow, who found in him much that was in common with his own nature. Borrow has left a dependable record of a meeting which took place between them at his Oulton home, during the Christmas of 1842. "He stayed with me during the greater part of the morning, discoursing on the affairs of Egypt, the aspect of which, he assured me, was becoming daily worse and worse. There is no living for the poor people, brother, said he, the chokengres (police) pursue us from place to place, and the gorgios are become either so poor or miserly, that they grudge our cattle a bite of grass by the wayside, and ourselves a yard of ground to light a fire upon. Unless times alter, brother, and of that I see no probability, unless you are made either poknees or mecralliskoe geiro (Justice of the Peace or Prime Minister), I am afraid the poor persons will have to give up wandering altogether, and then what will become of them?"

Yet there was much of Borrow's nature that was in common with that of Jasper Petulengro. Often the swarthy, horse-dealing gipsy was the mouthpiece through which he breathed forth his own abhorrence of conventional restraints and the thronging crowds of busy streets. He loved the open air country life that he lived near the Suffolk coast, where the fresh salt winds sweep up from the sea across gorse-clad denes and pleasant pasture-lands. He was happiest when amongst the "summer saturated heathen" of the heath and glen. Who can doubt that the much-quoted conversation in the twenty-fifth chapter of "Lavengro," gives expression to much of Borrow's own philosophy?

"Life is sweet, brother."

"Do you think so?"

"Think so! There's night and day, brother, both sweet things; sun, moon and stars, brother, all sweet things; there's likewise a wind on the heath. Life is very sweet, brother; who would wish to die?"

"I would wish to die?"

"You talk like a gorgio—which is the same as talking like a fool—were you a Romany chal you would talk wiser. Wish to die, indeed! A Romany chal would wish to live for ever!"

"In sickness, Jasper?"

"There's the sun and stars, brother."

"In blindness, Jasper?"

"There's the wind on the heath, brother; if I could only feel that, I would gladly live for ever."

Like Bamfylde Moore Carew, though for a different reason, it was to the gipsy life that Borrow turned after his unsuccessful literary work in London. Disappointed and despondent, he fled the scenes that had witnessed his failures. It is easy to imagine how great must have been his sense of freedom when he cast off the shackles of city life, and breathed again the air of the hills and pine-woods of rural England. With the poet whose bones rest in the midst of the little town of his birth, he felt and all his life maintained, that

> "'Tis liberty alone that gives the flower
> Of fleeting life its lustre and perfume,
> And we are weeds without it. All constraint,

Except what wisdom lays on evil men,
Is evil; hurts the faculties, impedes
Their progress in the road of science; blinds
The eyesight of discovery, and begets
In those that suffer it, a sordid mind
Bestial, a meagre intellect, unfit
To be the tenant of man's noble form."

The gipsies of the first quarter of the present century possessed the distinctive characteristics of their type in a far more marked degree than their descendants of to-day. There were few amongst them who had not a fair knowledge of the old Romany tongue, though they were utterly ignorant of its source. Questioned as to where their ancestors came from, they would tell you Egypt; and "business of Egypt" was their name for the mysteries of fortune-telling, and the other questionable proceedings they engaged in. Several of their families were fairly well-to-do in the eyes of their tribe, though the fact was carefully concealed from inquisitive gorgios. Often a gipsy *gry-engro*, or horse-dealer, would have a score or more horses on his hands at a time, while, not infrequently, his sales on a fair-day would amount to £50 or £60. The women of his camp would be gaudily and expensively dressed, and bedecked in heavy gold jewelry: he, himself, would often spend five or six pounds on a suit of clothes, and half a guinea on a silk handkerchief for his neck. Few of the women ever thought of marrying out of the Romany tribe, and their virtue and constancy were an example to all classes of society.

This last-mentioned fact is the more striking in view of the intense admiration often felt for the handsome *chis* by men who were not of the gipsy race. Commenting upon it not long ago, [77] an *Athenæum* reviewer said: "Between some Englishmen and gipsy women there is an extraordinary attraction—an attraction, we may say in passing, which did not exist between Borrow and the gipsy women with whom he was brought into contact. Supposing Borrow to have been physically drawn to any woman, she would have been of the Scandinavian type; she would have been what he used to call a Brynhild. It was tall blondes he really admired. Hence, notwithstanding his love of the economies of gipsy life, his gipsy women are all mere scenic characters, they clothe and beautify the scene: they are not dramatic characters. When he comes to delineate a heroine, Isopel Bernes, she is physically the very opposite of the Romany *chi*—a Scandinavian Brynhild, in short."

Mr. Watts has remarked on Borrow's neglect to portray the higher traits in the gipsy woman's character. Mrs. Herne and her grandchild Leonora, who are instanced as the two great successes of his Romany group, are both steeped in wickedness, and by omitting to draw a picture of the women's loftier side, he is said to have failed to demonstrate their great claim for distinction. There is a good deal of truth in this accusation; and yet it cannot be admitted wholly justifiable. In "The Romany Rye" we have a whole chapter devoted to the emphasising of the chastity of the Romany girls, and their self-sacrificing devotion to their husbands. Ursula marries a lazy, good-for-nothing *chal*, and then expressess her willingness to steal and swindle in order to keep him in comfort. The method is not commendable, but the object that prompts it is highly praiseworthy—from a Romany point of view.

But to-day the old race of genuine Romanies is fast dying out, and soon we shall have wholly lost the traces of a people who for many centuries have constituted a familiar feature of English country life. One of the last surviving *chals* of an old East Anglian gipsy family, in reply to a remark of the writer said, not long ago, "Yes, it is quite true that the old race of gipsies is dying out; there are very few of the real old Romanies to be met with at the present day. 'Mumpers' there are in plenty; folks who sell baskets and peddle clothes-pegs; but they are not of the true gipsy breed. At one time a gipsy never married out of his or her own tribe; but that day has gone, and there has been reared a mixed race with little of the true blood in them. Marrying into the 'mumping' and house-dwelling families has brought this about, and soon there will be no true Romanies left. Here and there you may meet a few, such as the Grays, Lees, and Coopers, and one or two of the Pinfolds; but they, too, are going the way of the rest. Yes, as you say, it is a pity, for after all the Romanies are a strange people, and, bad as they may have been, they were not without their good points. They knew a good horse when they saw one, and they let people see how a man, if he chooses, can shift for himself, without being beholden to any one. Anyhow, they have given clever men something to puzzle their brains about, and their language is not, as some would have it, a mere thieves 'patter,' but is a good, if not a better one, than that which the clever men speak themselves."

"Yes," went on my Romany friend, "this old language seems to interest a good many of the clever men. I have known some of them come to our tents and vans and write down the words and their meaning as we told them. I did not mind their doing it; but some of my people did not like it, and told them lies, and put them off with all sorts of queer stories. They were afraid the men should put the words into their books, and then it might be awkward for the gipsies when they wished to have a little talk amongst themselves on matters that were nobody's business but their own. Very few of the gipsies can read, so they did not learn the language in that way; most of us who know anything of it picked it up from our fathers and mothers when we were young. My father used to teach me certain sayings about horses that were very useful when we were dealing at the fairs. Now, however, some people who are not gipsies know more about these things than we do ourselves."

Footnotes:

[41] "The Zincali; or, An Account of the Gipsies of Spain," issued in two volumes in 1841.

[45] This is the name that was given to a small inlet during Borrows residence at Oulton. To-day it is sometimes called Burrough's Ham.

[77] *Athenæum*, March 28, 1896.